Praise for *The Phoenix Requires Ashes*

"If I had to use one word to describe Maureen Sandra Kane's fine poetry, it would be "elemental." Kane has the ability to boil down what's important in life to its essence, to boil the bones and use the elixir as if reading the tea leaves of the soul. Often she uses the elements in a space beyond metaphor. A fox here. A leaf there. Even tin foil crinkles open to reveal the heart. Her poetry will haunt your dreams. You have been warned." —Bliss Goldstein, MLA. Founding editor of *Tangents* magazine, Stanford University; winner of Sue C. Boynton Prize, 2022.

"Here in *The Phoenix Requires Ashes*, Maureen Kane reaches the soul of that which cannot be easily named and puts words to the longing for connection with our secret truths. Yes, in these pages, "deep calls to deep." Read with an open heart and you will find your own shadow, your own grief, your own hope, and ultimately, your own resilience. Every poem is a beautiful acknowledgement of what it means to be a human whose full complexity deserves to be mined."
—Cami Osman, author of *Second Wind: One Woman's Midlife Quest to Run Seven Marathons on Seven Continents*.

"Maureen Sandra Kane makes exquisite use of the images of her Pacific Northwest milieu. Her work can be as earthy as Pablo Neruda's, or as ethereal as Richard Bach's. The process of realizing who one is, as laid out in the pages of this volume, becomes more appealing and less painful with this guidebook. You will meditate on Kane's words long after you finish reading them." —Seán Dwyer, author of *A Quest for Tears: Surviving Traumatic Brain Injury*.

The Phoenix Requires Ashes

Poems for the Journey

MAUREEN SANDRA KANE

Gray Matter Press
Seattle Los Angeles

Copyright © 2022 by Maureen Kane

All rights reserved. No part of this publication may be reproduced, distributed, or transmitted in any form or by any means, including photocopying, recording, or other electronic or mechanical methods, without the prior written permission of the publisher, except in the case of brief quotations embodied in critical reviews and certain other noncommercial uses permitted by copyright law. For permission requests, write to the publisher, addressed "Attention: Permissions," at the website below.

Gray Matter Press

The Brain Initiative, Inc.

www.the-brain-initiative.com

ISBN: 8-9862415-0-0
ISBN-13: 979-8-9862415-0-0

The Phoenix Requires Ashes: Poems for the Journey
Maureen Sandra Kane 1st ed.

Cover painting by Suzanne Wynne. Used by permission.
Book design and cover design by Seán Dwyer.

Dedication:

Thank you to Ellison, Barb, Karen, and Janet, who witnessed the birth of my first poem and encouraged me to write. To Karen Frances, for hours of feedback and conversation. To Mirabai, who was the doula to many of the thoughts expressed here, and to my husband and best friend, Sean, who heartily supports any goal I think of.

Contents

Let Yourself Be Weary 1
Seasonal Zen 2
Change 4
Hollow Bone 5
Silence 6
Midlife Elements 8
The Moon Won't Use the Door 9
Quan Yin Is My Co-Therapist 10
First the Sorrow 12
Only Writing Does Writing 14
"Only writing does writing – everything else is gone." 14
Packing for Home 15
Meditation 16
Kitchen Floor 17
Shabbat Candle Holder 18
Porcelain Doll 19
Get Your Story Straight 20
Madrona 21
Cycles Back Home 23
Sea Turtle 24
The Rigging 26
Acceptance, Except… 27
Therapist's Entreaty 28
Guide 29
Crowbar 31

Peace in the Eye of the Storm	33
A Prayer for Those Without Words	35
Two States	37
This Apple	38
Quilt Museum	40
The Forgotten War Memorial	44
Injustice	46
Warrior	47
In Praise of Introverts	49
Winter	50
Vignettes of Kindness	51
2am Christmas	53
Dancing with My Body	54
Look Up	55
That Unnoticed and That Necessary	57
Closed Doorway	58
Timelines	59
Her Body Speaks	61
Yes	62
Authenticity	64
Remember	66
Finds Joy	68
Reimagining Wild Things	70
Citations	72
Acknowledgments	73
ABOUT THE AUTHOR	75

The Phoenix Requires Ashes

Let Yourself Be Weary

Let your body crumble to the ground
and lie on the wet forest floor.
Right here, in the middle of your path.

Let your skin and bones slide off your soul
surrendering dreams and hopes,
and to-do lists
into the decaying leaves and rich soil.

Give yourself to roots and mushrooms.

Let yourself become nurse log
molting snake
earthworm, digesting dirt.
Join the ants in their underground labyrinths.
Sleep cozily with rabbit and fox beneath the earth.

Let your weariness be the chrysalis holding
your bare beating heart and soul.

rest, and rest, and rest

And from here, let your life renew.
Breathe and wait
until you have some recognition
of who you have become

Seasonal Zen

Spring explodes in almost painful colors
like bright posterboards holding children's presentations.
"Look at me!"
"No, look at me!"
Butterflies and hummingbirds hardly know
where to perch first.
Gently seasons turn.
Leaves brown, thin,
and only the spiderweb skeletons remain.
Black-eyed Susans' bee-stripe costumes drop,
leaving sticks, and haunted bones.
This piques my interest.
What remains when color rests,
without the distraction of paint and noise?
Perhaps this is where truth resides.

Photo credit: Carol Kilgore

Photo credit: Carol Kilgore

Change

What I know is story, tradition, interpretation.
What I don't know is truth.

The story is a costume I zip up
making sure the hood is tight over my head.
Without it I am raw and confused, unprotected.

How does the snake know it is safe when it molts?
Is it afraid?
Does the butterfly pupa have consciousness?
Are the imaginal cells worried?
I mean, it can take months, even years, for them to
 transform.

What about the moment when a hermit crab changes
 shells?
It seems we are designed to be vulnerable when we grow.
How do we know we will be ok?
Is not knowing part of the design?
Terror must be a mistake of evolution.

I would like to bottle snake, pupa, and crab courage.
Just as paper is not paper, but made of sunlight..and
 rain..and dirt..and sky,
Perhaps change and terror are made of
trust
patience
time
surrender
and transformation.

Hollow Bone

Inside the hollow bone
dusty, empty,
breath sweeps through but finds no purchase.
What life was there?
What loss?

Inside the hollow bone
Breath asks,
What life is here?
What longs for nurture?

Inside the hollow bone
the lost one says,
Maybe,
but not today.

Inside the hollow bone
Presence says,
Tell me.
Tell me your fear, your terror, your pain
that imprisons you in this wasteland.

Inside the hollow bone
the lost one wonders,
Can she exist?
Is she not too much?
Would not the world be decimated if she spoke her truth?
Can she bear disappointment again?

For today, presence and the lost one
rest together uneasily
inside the hollow bone.

Silence

I tried to write a poem about trusting our path
by writing about bumpers in bowling alleys.
I wrote about stinky shoes, and hotdogs,
and children leaning with all their might,
urging the ball to arc to their will.

I tried to convey the unseen greater meaning in our lives
with endless words about dropping rocks into ponds.
Ripples that flow from our actions.
I stopped when the words *pay it forward* flowed from my
   pen.

I ache to reach into my depths
and pull up what I need to say,
need to hear.
That ineffable bubbling of Spirit into my spirit,
into the pen.

Life-changing wisdom
that will stop the reader
and compel her to read it three times,
fold it up and put it in her heart,
and face the world renewed.

I want to write the poem that will tilt the world
towards love so that path is downhill, not up.
I need the words to make sense of pain
and glorify the meaning we make from tragedy.
The ways we keep going
even when we are sure we can't.

I need verses that see the unseen
and adorn the lonely
in friendship and comfort.

I desperately need a sonnet to heal divides
and restore our brokenness.
I want my writing to flow into the gold Kintsugi,*
making a vessel large enough to hold us all.

Today, all I have are bowling alleys and bumpers.

And silence.

*The art of putting broken pottery pieces back together
with gold, built on the idea that embracing flaws creates
stronger and more beautiful art.

Midlife Elements

Burning fire climbs from the belly and bursts out of the head.
Flames lick the face.
Not sure if this time it will consume everything.
Unstoppable power
cleansing everything in its path,
burns the underbrush and singes old growth.

It does not stop to ask questions
or permission.
Only the relentless chant *I AM HERE*.
Stop everything.
I AM HERE.

Bow to my power and strength.
I am the phoenix and the ashes.
I anoint you into fire,
and relentlessness,
and power.

Take stock
there is no longer time for mediocrity.
What needs to burn down?
What needs to rise?

And then it passes.
And the waterfall comes
leaving us shivering and wet.

The Moon Won't Use the Door

> *"The moon won't use the door, only the window"*
> -RUMI

Oh how I prefer the door
with its square and predictable edges.
That satisfying click that tells me the task is finished.
The solid, unchangeable wood.
The moon, the window, their magic
while luminous—so inaccessible to my understanding of language.
Can it not give me words, comfort, directions,
the rewarding click of surety?
How am I to follow glimmers and reflections and give up solidity?
And yet, the moon will outlast the door – that is sure.

Quan Yin Is My Co-Therapist

Sitting atop her fiery dragons
legs gently crossed in a languid lotus.
Soft hands,
one holding medicine
the other in the mudra of patience.
Jewels around her neck.

Her face in deep peace, eyes half-mast
introspective with a hint of smile.
She who receives the pain of others remains undisturbed,
Embodied, she can hold it all.

I see her image when I am unsure,
and I let her hold us.
Therapist and client
held patiently in her field.
Together we watch as the medicine reveals itself.

Photo by Maureen Sandra Kane

First the Sorrow

Let it creak and moan
Let it rise and flood your body
until it feels you might drown.
Just move a little.
You can breathe.
You are still here.

Let it rise.
Let it rise.

Want nothing else.
Trust the pain
and find your thread to weave into a shawl
made from strands of the ones who came before.
You are not lost.

They know this pain
this river of sorrow.

Gather your ancestors, your elders
their fires and funeral pyres.
Their chanting and wailing holds yours.

They know how.

Let it rise.
Let it rise.

For after the flood
comes a trickle of joy
then a stream.
Because streams never stop.

You will join the dancers, your heart open and empty
ready to receive.
You, a rock, rubbed smooth and bright by the water you
    could not stop,
inhabiting your own life.

But first the sorrow.

Only Writing Does Writing

> *"Only writing does writing — everything else is gone."*
> -NATALIE GOLDBERG

Breath breathes.
The run runs the runner.
Truth tells truth.
Flow flows the water.
Creativity creates.
Yet,
Beauty is in the I of the beholder.

Packing for Home

Most of my time I've been leaving.
Dropping it all to find a better place.
Leaving behind parts of me and mine.
Now I travel to find them again.

Wandering far and wide to gather
all the things I left behind.
Things I didn't think I wanted any more.
Things I thought I might need in that location again.
Shabby teddy bears, chewed-up cat toys
hold history I love, but tossed aside.

Sorting my lamps from their lamps.
Choosing whose light I follow.
Sorting and bundling.
Packing in old suitcases, boxes,
whatever can hold it.
And bringing it home.

Meditation

Breath
Rain
Cat
Birds
Sadness
To-do list

Kitchen Floor

What if I could sweep with delight?
Peer deeply into detritus
to see a microcosm of visitors.
Like how sand under a microscope becomes shells again.
To gather and honor, not just discard.
How many venerated guests have I thrown away?
Remnants of dinners shared together,
cat litter from the old kitty who pains to use the box,
maple leaves from the peaceful refuge of backyard
   sanctuary.
All here to bring awareness to the macro in the micro
in their quiet, unassuming way.
What if every thing could be this delightful
in its own being
as it does nothing but lie silently on the ground?

Shabbat Candle Holder

How does one distill a culture,
a history,
massacre,
survival and faith
into a mass-produced candelabrum?

The hands of my grandmother and mother lit and prayed
and polished here.
Patina and wax witness the years and prayers
born of pain and joy.

If I do not carry the tradition, where does that leave the
    lineage?
Have I shirked my duty,
or is it just a candle holder
and I am the lineage?

Porcelain Doll

Her name is Big Baby.
There is a little baby, but she is plastic and never seemed
 real.
Big Baby's eyes can blink...what a wonder!
First loved by my grandmother
then my mother
then by me.
Recipient of all our young maternal attention.
Rocked and rubbed smooth by little girls creating family.
Dressed in my brother's infant onesie.
Her cracked fingers and dislocated shoulder do not
 diminish
her sweet and silent presence.
Quietly waiting to meet the needs of a little girl.

Get Your Story Straight

My legacy is of love and fear.
Run.
Don't move.
Hide.
I didn't know that worry was love in disguise.
Neither did she and hers.
I didn't know that lack of empathy was encouragement incognito.
Neither did he and his.
So my legacy was paralysis.
Yet some part of me persists in fits and starts, tangling with itself
often in fear
it stumbles forward.
Our long-reaching legacy is of survival, vision, education, and persistence.
That strength, a through-line of our salvation.

Madrona

Outside the window of the little old cabin
a madrona stands, spreading her branches proudly as she
 watches the cove below.
Perhaps she is over 100 years old; she can live 200 years.
Studying this scene, I begin pondering the second half of
 my life.

I believe I would like to be a Madrona in my remaining
 years:
Comfortable on the edge,
holding fast to the earth without concern for falling.
Knowing how to shed my skin for growth.
Welcoming wind and storms because I need them
 to become strong.
Embracing soft, exposed flesh,
trusting that new bark always comes.
Growing towards the light wherever it is.

Built to survive where planted,
No longer waiting "for it to be over."
Standing still at cliff's edge, embracing nobility in sunshine,
or downpours, unmoving,
birds purchased in my limbs.

Seeds and fruit released without effort
for visitors who carry them away,
bearing fruit I will never see.
Falling leaves taking disease as they go.

No worries about being enough or having enough,
no words even for enough,
because I am enough.
There is more than enough.

Saint Madrone of Barcelona,
the patron saint of horticulture who brings rain.
May my life bring nourishing rain,
graceful and noble strength,
with a deep knowing that both sun and storms sustain.

Cycles Back Home

First you follow the leader.
They say you'll be ok,
and you need them to say this.
Life changes.
They leave.
You leave.
Another ritual. Another New Year.
All in hopes of changing the outcome.
Which Vessel?
Which Candle?
Which prayer will make it ok?
Then one day your past meets you again.
You watch with pride.
They say you'll be ok.
This time, standing alone,
You know you are.

Sea Turtle

I had never seen a sea turtle in real life
before I had that vision.

The doctor said this mass is of concern
and offered Xanax
while I waited the weeks before a mammogram
    appointment.

Being young, I'd never had a mammogram before,
let alone something *of concern.*
Every night, I sat in bed and googled breast cancer
    symptoms.
And tried to feel if my lump matched
Web MD
or Health News Today
or Providence.org.

It was a little like breastcancer.org described,
but not like what Mayo Clinic said,
a lot like cancer.gov though.

Rocking back and forth, alone in my room
panic rising,
I thought about how I would handle chemo
living by myself.

I prayed every night for comfort and health.

During work, I snuck in web searches for
benign lumps
does breast cancer go away on its own?
How do you know if it's cancer or just a cyst?

One morning, out of the blue,
I had a vision of a languid sea turtle
lazily gliding in sunlit waters
Held afloat in the bright blue-green ocean without effort,
flippers aloft as she drifted by.

She looked me in the eye as she floated,
sunbeams streaming down around her,
lighting up her green carapace.

Without words, I knew it was going to be ok.
And it was.

Today, a little clay sea turtle sits on my desk.
Sometimes my eye catches hers
just when I need her medicine.

She is sparkly purple
with a laughing grin on her face.

Her head cocked upwards, just so
her left eye looks right at me.

Each time I notice her,
it's a surprise.
And I'm reminded once again
that all is well, regardless of the results.

The Rigging

> *"Life is Rigged for the Good"*
> -NEIL ALLEN

Heron stands patiently watching the water.
He knows the fish will come.
Exposed, he is graceful, still, straight-backed he waits.
He stands *in* the water, dives right in.
The fish come.
Sometimes the fish don't come,
but mostly they do.

Hummingbird buzzes and weaves
between madrona branches in inexplicable flight.
Hovering and flashing neon pink, red, purple.
Predators and mates both can see those colors.
He trusts that it's worth it.
Using all that energy, then drinks for only a moment and is
    off again.
He could stay still and drink his fill,
but he knows nectar abounds today.
Sometimes nectar isn't there, so he slows himself,
but mostly it is.

Ancient Madrona reaches over the bluff,
anchored in scree and rock.
Wind buffets, and Madrona is content.
Sunlight and water come.
Trees are made to create the very rain they need.
The cliff holds fast. Sometimes it doesn't,
but mostly it does.

Acceptance, Except...

> *"Only when you have no more need for acceptance,
> will everything you do be accepted."*
> -RUMI

I accept pain,
except my own.
And I wish to ease yours.
I accept disappointment,
except for those I love.
I accept death,
except when I don't.
Can acceptance have conditions?
Are there degrees of acceptance?
If there are, I have a GED, maybe a high school diploma.
I can completely accept that I struggle to accept.
I have a Master's degree in this.
Yet this acceptance of the struggle is a softening, and that
    matters.
I can accept that we suffer, as long as I can find a meaning
or narrative as the prize.
I can accept that not accepting injustice gives me the
power and energy to fight.
Who would I be in full acceptance?
Where would the fight come from then?
I think that this space is the one that could heal the world.
I'll let you know when I get there.

Therapist's Entreaty

The soul enters the class VI rapids, and while the rest must follow, we fight.
Instinct fights
Rails
"No!"
"Why?"
How do we hold the truth that it will be worse?
Can we hold onto resilience?
How must we navigate the rapids when the end is certain?
What do we do in the respite of the calmer pools,
when we know they are temporary?
We yell to the gods, but our voices are lost in the din.
Every soul arrives here one day.
What sustains us then?
And how do I bottle it for others?

Guide

Sun shines bright on the bay radiating towards the street.
Boats glide by.
People stroll along the road towards the water.

Crash.
Body crushed and rattled.
It all changes.
Involuntary descent to Elysium[1].

No one goes on purpose, but all must go sometime.
There, it is required to feel
abandoned,
discarded,
broken,
hopeless.
Without this, there is no ascent.

The phoenix required ashes.
The butterfly needed imaginal discs and goo.
You, a car.

Your ascent required
community,
fortitude,
vision,
authoring,
re-authoring.

You will visit Elysium from time to time,
But the roadmap home has been assimilated through
acceptance,
pain,
and time.

You, Charon[2], and Inanna[3] have made peace.
Now, you escort others.

[1]The land of afterlife in Greek Mythology/The Underworld

[2]Ferryman to the Underworld

[3]Goddess who ascended from the Underworld after many trials

Crowbar

I watch you get in your car to drive away to new
destinations and adventures.
Towards the dreams that make your life worthwhile,
exciting and interesting.

And yet, years ago, on a simple drive,
You almost didn't live.

So, you go out into the world to expand your life
and my heart contracts,
crumples like aluminum foil crushed into a ball.

I see your crumpled car, half its size,
the back seat now part of the front.
Glass in the street.
I hear the police officer telling me that cars are meant to
fold like that.
Trying to take solace in those words.

I see myself at the impound yard
asking the worker for a crowbar to open the door
so I can look for your wallet,
And I watch glass pour out of every opening we make.

I remember the confusion and pain of the years of
    recovery.
The excruciating pain of sunlight in your eyes,
You showing the waitress a photo of your accident
because you can't find the words for how you want your
    eggs.
The daily naps you still need.

I think about the terror I felt each time you threatened to quit your job
because it is so hard to work,
knowing we'd be left without health insurance.
I see you age and deny this reality.

All I want is for you to just stay with me
in safety, and companionship, and quiet.
Play a game, watch a fire, point at a bird, share a meal.

But that is not who you are.
Not who I married.

Slowly I reach into my crinkled aluminum foil heart
and pry apart a few edges
to make some room for your dreams.
A little glass falls out.

Peace in the Eye of the Storm

I wake to find a newborn fawn on my front doorstep.
Really.
Her soft downy form curled in a circle,
sleeping peacefully, knowing her mother will return.
Brown hairs fluttering in the wind,
the tiny white spots rise and fall with her breath.
She is unafraid and resting with complete trust.

She may see, but does not understand
the work of neighbors to keep her safe.
Traffic cones placed to keep people away,
Signs redirecting package deliveries, and
our choice to let the lawn grow
until the fawn is ready to move out on her own.

She does not know when she suckles
that her milk contains apples and pears we left out
    for her mother
who wanders to lead predators away.

In our back yard, a rare black squirrel swings from
    the bird feeder
sharing the food carefully curated for our local
    avian guests.

This pastoral scene all around me
teaches of innate trust, care, and grace.
We humans may be recipients of it too,
in ways we will never see or understand,
just as the fawn knows not what keeps her safe.

Meanwhile a pandemic continues to rage.
Hoarding and choices about mask use spark fear,
division, and violence.

Some seek to escalate the division for their own gain.

And yet, the helpless fawn trusts
and is protected.

Tonight, we will watch a rabbit bring grass and sticks
one by one into her burrow in the front yard,
to house her young.
We will text the neighbors,
and once again watch over a little one the best we can.

We humans,
who pretend we are not helpless,
could learn a lot from what mightiness
one tiny life brings out in those around her,
through her innocence and trust.

May all beings meet their innate greatness
which rises to meet our vulnerability.

Photo by Seán Dwyer

A Prayer for Those Without Words

> *"Praying...Patch a few words together and don't try to make them elaborate, this isn't a contest but the doorway."*
> -MARY OLIVER

For the little ones who only know pain
and don't know prayer.
For the tears they turn on themselves,
for the false stories, made solid and real
and unshakable
in order to survive.

For the big ones trapped in trauma.
The ones who see it and can't move.
And the ones who don't,
but act it out on others.

For the stuck, the hurting, the blind
I pray.
For the pain, the twisted survival
I pray.
For the strength, grace, and resilience
I pray.

For those who have the courage to sit in despair,
the monks who go to caves to cry for humankind,
fill their wells.

For the children who cry and blame themselves,
empty their wells.
For the earth,
clean her wells.
For the helpless, the hopeless, the trying, and the
    constrained,
bring them water.

Let us cry and release.
Let us drink anew and transform,
I pray.

Two States

Physics says an object cannot exist in the same place in two different states,
but that is not true for me today.

My feet stick in the mud as I move through fog towards the woods,
tired, sore, weary,
but determined to shift my state.
The words of Howard Therman in my earbuds,
in hopes of soothing mind, soul, and body.

In the quiet forest, moss drips from branches,
water drips from moss,
making pleasing dense plucking sounds on the ground.

The air is thick and slow.
The grove timeless.
Branches twist, and trees look like ancient Seussian creatures
quietly waiting and blessing life.

I try to pay attention, be mindful.
But thoughts stray to the to-do list,
the things I can't control, and the discomfort and fears in my body.

So we co-exist,
me in my state and the forest in its.
And that is enough for me.

I exit the forest in acceptance
and pass an old, empty, rusty truck,
motor off,
windshield wiper blades moving slowly back and forth.

This Apple

This red apple in my hand.
Cool and firm, with specks of green.
Ready for a crisp bite with my strong teeth,
or a sweet pie,
or to become sauce in my larder.

Simply an apple, but also:
Sun, and seed dropped by birds.
Warm tilled earth and earthworms.
Mycelium feeding and talking to the growing tree.
The underground World Wide Web sharing nutrients and
warning of viruses.

The orchardist creating conditions for growth
carefully protecting and pruning.
Night school to learn about disease, and taxes, and organic
    certifications.

The harvester feeding his family, toiling in sun and rain
his years of expertise and the sacrifice of his body.

They who designed the roads, built the roads, maintain the
roads for those who drive the shipping trucks.
Do we need to think about the invention of the internal
    combustion engine?

The teen who stocks store shelves at night, counting
paychecks until the next fashion drop.
The customer who picked up my apple,
but chose another and left it for me to find.
The checkout clerk who celebrated her grandmother's 90th
birthday last night with ice cream,
because if you are old enough, who cares if you eat ice
    cream.

My paycheck, earned by helping others, who then help others…

What a miracle, this apple in my hand.
So many hands it took to arrive.

Can I make a pie worthy of this blessing?

Quilt Museum

My heart quickens to discover it's a Victorian house with
　　two turrets.
Grey and green and yellow,
with a touch of mauve in just the right places,
suggesting both stateliness and whimsy.
I immediately pick out which turret would be my
　　bedroom.

Pine stairs creak beneath our feet as we walk through the
archways to the porch.
I don't think the arches have any purpose
except for beauty,
and the perfect place for yellow accent paint.

Inside, we are greeted by an elder in a bonnet
who tells us she's been there since the beginning.
She happily shows us photos and books,
and secrets of the house.
The narrow servants' stairs, the butler's pantry now the
　　staff lounge,
and photos of a fire the house endured.
Wherever we turn, she is there,
thrilled to make our visit interesting.

Quilts cut from 100-year-old paper adorn the first floor,
no photography here please.
Around the corner, faded nine patch, log cabin,
　　and crazy quilts
in pastel Easter-egg colors.
Perfectly straight lines and patterns seamlessly align,
while I struggle with my balance on the uneven flooring.

I ponder the time and effort, hand stitching them just so,
perhaps while sharing stories, grief, and triumphs

of the sisterhood who made them.
I wonder what the women did when their eyes grew old
    and tired,
their fingers arthritic.
I think they kept quilting.

Up the stairs,
the wild cacophony begins.
Peacock feathers leap out of fabric,
intricate and ornate fine, fuzzy tendrils jump out into the
    third dimension.
A conductor waves his wand to fabric music notes blasting
off the canvas.
Lilies wave in sunlit fields.

Turtles swim slowly through swirling stitches of a
turquoise ocean.
A couple reclines in a deck chair, watching children play
on the beach.
How on earth does someone paint this picture with bits of
    fabric?
Spiderwebs, butterflies, sunsets, cityscapes,
all leap from the minds of their artists into the fibers.

One piece is a memorial
to all whom we have lost through Covid.
Simply the shape of a smile,
repeated hundreds of times
to commemorate all the smiles we have lost.
It takes up an entire wall.
A jarring pause in the delight of colors in the other rooms.

Up one more floor, I find the turreted room I claimed
    upon entry.

There are no quilts here,
Just an exquisite raw chevron floor built around an 1891
    landmark seal.
Crowned with trompe-l'œil ceiling of sky and clouds,
a small antique crib rests by the bay window
looking over the city with pride and stature.

Back down the rasping stairs,
we make our way to the gift shop
and purchase a scarlet kimono
to wear in our bedroom
that does not have quilts either.

The Forgotten War Memorial

19 men in stainless steel ponchos,
faces frozen in horror,
emerge from the trees
trudge through bushes and swamp.
Rifles on backs and shoulders, and in hands.

On perpetual patrol,
their eyes follow you.

They look like ghosts
exhausted, pale,
haunted by what they have seen
what they've done
whom they have lost.
Weary bodies, tight, vigilant.

Photo by Jan Dommerholt on Unsplash

Standing for 19 branches and each combat job, the men reflect off a black wall
where ghostly images of clergy, code breakers, nurses, pilots, and even dogs, float but cannot escape.

Nearly five million dead or missing.
Those who returned
came back to Americans distracted by the inventions of color TV,
Playboy, and Disneyland.
And took their place as ghosts in society.

The epitaph reads
"Freedom is not Free."

Injustice

This is where they want us.
Too tired to sleep.
Weary,
tears are too much work.

Throbbing face.
Fossilized shoulders.
Petrified being.

There used to be anger
Fear.
Grief.
Now, the mere idea of taking out garbage, or flossing,
is too much.
Can't even visualize the next step,
let alone take it.

Defeated.
Deflated.
Why bother.

Staring at the phone while humanity drains away.
Alone.

Warrior

I don't want to be resilient any longer.
Can't.
Shouldn't have to be.
And yet I do
have to be.

Because injustice, climate change, and illness are resilient
 too.

A wise friend told me to shift my idea of what resilience is.
That it is not a verb I *do*,
with limited capacity,
which gets used up.

Rather, it is an ineffable something that rises to meet the
 day.
Flames my outrage,
spurs me to act.
And says,
This is not over.
There is enough.
Be patient.
Be loud.
Be what is called for,
You can do this.

Inextinguishable
Unquenchable
Irrepressible
Enduring
Ebullient
Everlasting

This thing,
that words can only point towards, but cannot pin down,
sings the singer
writes the poem
organizes the protest
calls the doctor, again.

Tucks me into bed at night
kisses my forehead and says,
rest, we'll do more tomorrow.

And waits beside me while I sleep.

In Praise of Introverts

In a world so loud and boastful,
where the whitest, most confident blaring voice
wins leadership and trust,
our planet falters.
Wars are waged
and new ideas suffocated.

In a world where billionaires justify their worth through
    pissing contests
over whose phallic rocket goes the farthest,
gentleness and thoughtfulness are drowned out.

Praise for the lowly introvert.
She who is immune to the lures of fame and attention.
He who thinks, and reasons, reaches deep inside,
and pulls up innovation from his depths.

Would that we could invert this hierarchical pyramid
of mansplaining, obscene grabs for attention, and noise.

Upright the grounded base and say:
shhhhh boastful ones,
have a nap.
Choose your juice box and blankie.
The rest of us will fix your mess.

Winter

Yesterday there was color and light
and lines.
Headlights streamed across the dark horizon.
Christmas lights shone into the water across the bay
Wavy, bright red, green, and yellow flashes told my eye
This is where the background stops.
Ducks go in the middle ground
stars are in the sky,
and you, my friend, are the observer in the foreground.

This is how we follow the rules.

Today there is only softness and curves.
White on white on white.
There is no longer water, or sky, or road.
Horizontal and vertical cease to be.
Only velvet, downy, foggy stillness.

Black birds float on white fluffy clouds where the water
 used to be.
Diving beneath and reappearing, making no ripples.
Dark dots of fowl forming lines and shapes
spelling words in an alphabet I don't know.

Today the only rules are
coziness, mistiness
nestled, and held…. In curves.

I am ensconced in softness and silence.
One solitary red bird pecking near my feet.

Vignettes of Kindness

The physical therapist guides me through positions that
bring on vertigo
and changes her technique,
so she can hold my hand.
Her touch makes it almost bearable.

My loving, also conspiracy theorist, eye doctor
meets my fear of the procedure with cold compresses,
and waits patiently each time
until the panic ebbs.

The grocery clerk looks me in the eye
and actually does care how my day has been,
even though I just say fine.

The veterinarians cry with us
when it's time to say goodbye to our beloved cat.
Later they ceremoniously deliver her ashes to our house.

Neighbors prank us with holiday blowups all over our
    yard,
play so many game nights,
and rally for each other
from grocery runs to ER visits.
People we trust with our keys and our children.

The friend who shows up every Saturday for our walk
no matter the weather.

The hospital aide appears out of nowhere
to catch and whisk away vomit,
then disappears
before I even know what is happening.

The anesthesiologist hears I am afraid
and stops to do mindfulness with me
as the drugs take effect.

The nurses notice when I wake up
and reassure me that I'm ok.
My husband's voice and hand soothe me.

The doctor takes time to appeal to the insurance company three times,
and shares my outrage at the injustice.

My husband's children ask if their children can call me
    Grandma.

2am Christmas

"What do you need?" he asks
before she can request.
He lies down to comfort her.
Cool hands hold clammy ones.
Solidity meets shaking.
"What do I do?" she asks.
"Ride it out, I'm here," he says.
She calms.
Cat snuggles.
She finds gratitude and solace between
waves of pain.
Stillness enfolds.

Dancing with My Body

Brown bear dances, bottom heavy
grounded in the present.
Hummingbird dances,
Hollow-boned and flighty.
My body dances slowly, lithely,
often unoccupied.
Pain sends consciousness to hummingbird flight.
Experience sends consciousness to hide
and seek hollowness.
Dancing with my body.
Coming Home.

Look Up

> *"Be happy*
> *Make this day a tree*
> *Leaning over the river of eternity*
> *And fuss about on its branches."*
> -JIMMY SANTIAGO BACA

Look up, Madrona says.
You who notices the small, the beautiful,
the hidden on the ground,
under rocks,
in the creek bed.

A glint of color—lime seaweed between a sea of grey
 rocks.
Tiny shells resting inside an open clam like a swaddled
 baby,
tumbled in the ocean, yet still whole.
A shard of green beach glass,
one rust-colored rock.
How the purple mussels shine when wet.

You stoop to see.
Take a picture.
Photographed, the tiny scene becomes larger than life
creating a new world of possibilities hardly noticed before.
Breath quickens at the awe of it.

Resting at day's end,
your gaze follows the sleek, wet madrona trunks
gently curving towards the heavens.
Not until well ensconced in sky
does the canopy drape itself out into the ethers,
stretching like fingers and toes

a full-throated vinyasa
one movement flowing into the next.

Look up, Madrona says.
There is splendor you are missing.

That Unnoticed and That Necessary

> *"I would like to be the air that
> inhabits you for a moment only.
> I would like to be that unnoticed
> and that necessary."*
> -MARGARET ATWOOD, VARIATION ON THE WORD SLEEP

The way my essence seems to be what you need.
That our partings and parings require a kiss.
Knowing you will be there when I ask.
How many Doctors' waiting rooms have we sat in
 together?
Evenings, listening to the day's download,
clearing room for presence
at the end of the day.
Your neon socks with brown pants
because it tickles you.
Your antithetical love of spreadsheets, and music,
 and chaos,
and doing all the things at once.
My love for order.
How we both delight in absurdity.
It's a given – simply, we are.

Closed Doorway

Knocking at the door.
Pounding at the door.
Battering ram.
It won't open.
Sitting on the floor,
my tiny body leaning against the immense door towering
over the dark.
I see a crack of light underneath it.
I plead.
Sob.
Wait (maybe patience is the key).
It stays closed.
I use my tools: breath, challenging thoughts, compassion,
  journal.
It
will
not
open.
This suffering has to mean something to bear it.
It needs to lead somewhere to be worth it.
I need a prize.
What if the door is just an idea and there is nowhere to go?
Can I sit and sob here and not arrive anywhere?
What is the door?
My culture says it is required for successful transformation.
And that transformation is required too.
I think I will go to the woods with my wholeness,
where there are no doors.
And let the door fight itself.

Timelines

Every day brings some reminder that I am getting older.
Crepey skin that wasn't there just yesterday.
My mother's face in the mirror.
How my neck pops, creaks and complains so loudly,
without manners.
Small print is winning the war, so I let it say what it likes
like a child murmuring inaudibly under her breath while
rolling her eyes.
Vitamin bottles threaten to outnumber spice jars on the
    counter.

We talk about how many next pets we realistically can
    have.
We will have to know the lifespan of cats and birds and
    dogs.
What will it be like to adopt our last pet?

This great adventure of midlife
feels vulnerable,
and freeing too.

Before me I see two timelines.
The *Sliding Doors* of aging.

One door is growing old alone,
Trapped in illness and perhaps poverty.
Maybe in one of those homes that smell like urine.

The other is in the faces of elders around the world in
National Geographic, and *Time*, and Hollywood.
The mothers, and artists, and writers, and teachers.

Sometimes toothless, leathery skin.
But you will recognize them by their eyes.

Oh, those eyes!
Deep, dark (even if they are blue), smiling eyes
that have seen it all and still dance with aliveness and
     wisdom,
and most of all delight.

Eyes that say "this is not so bad, I've seen worse."
"Let's celebrate each other and this beautiful, catastrophic
     world."
Eyes that say "I know secrets you will discover if you just
     wait."
"Then, you will laugh with me too."

I humbly ask those elders to put their hands on my heart
and initiate me into their world.

Her Body Speaks

I speak for the sinew that pulls at my bones.
Red and raw – gaping and mawing.
Holding all together, the strength required astounds.
Willing to knit again if pulled too far.

Listen.
Listen to my cracking, straining, reshaping.
I do it for you, and you don't notice until I snap.
I speak for quiet awareness
where my fibers align, juices flow,
and symbiosis drives us forward.

I speak for the miracle that knits muscle to bone
and lets us dance.
Can you not see me as beautiful?

I speak for the curves and dimples that pad and feed the
    body,
badges earned from creating and sustaining life,
holding nourishment for the lean times.
I speak for the fat that keeps you warm,
cushions your falls,
and knows exactly when to hold, and when to release
    sustenance.
Can't you see me as nourishing you?

I speak for the wisdom of physicality,
the pulsing, beating, moving aliveness
that creates a body.
Your oldest companion.
May we make peace
so you can see my miracles?

Yes

If I wait long enough
I may find it.
Scan the body,
watch the breath,
notice thinking.

Watch the fear.
Try to tame the unknown into something I can control,
as if I were God today.

Surprised by the fragments of emotion triggered yesterday
and still with me.
Confused about what and whose emotion it even is.

Suddenly, without effort it may appear.
A small, shabby hut deep in my belly
arises from the fog.
Clad in grey peeling shingles,
no front porch, just old wooden steps to the grey door.
Deep in the woods
beside a moonlight lake.

You wouldn't think much of it,
but walk inside.
It is empty and abandoned
except for a well-worn rocking chair.

Sit and rock
and wait.
Listen to the chair creak
and the wood floor groan.

See the moon illuminate dancing dust motes
and feel the space become alive.

There is breath and rhythm, arising out of kindness,
and assurance that all is well.
Like a deep ocean holding the storms raging on its surface.
This is the engine of life, of my body.

No news headlines seeking my fear.
No divisions seeking my allegiance.
It is only deep, still interconnection.

My hut is not pure or sanctified like the golden temples.
No stained glass or icons.
It is dusty and dark, but more pure
than any shrine.

Wiser than any scripture,
its only message is a quiet "yes."

Authenticity

It seems to me that we on earth are meant to experience pleasure.
Life itself begins (when all things go well) from passion and delight.

There is no practical need for the beauty of flowers and sunsets,
the taste of ripe peaches,
but we have them here.
The smell of vanilla,
the feeling of grass underfoot,
are not needed for the survival of the species,
but are gifts.

Even "bad" feelings hold pleasure.
Allowing a pure, heartfelt sob evokes grace and compassion.
And come on, being mad feels good, doesn't it?

We teach our children to sit still,
deny their bodies,
feel shame when laughing, being loud, getting dirty, being curious.
Train them to fear feelings,
deny human needs.

We must produce,
be good,
earn our place.
We must hide and fear authenticity.

I propose a revolution.
Let's be authentic.
Notice and elevate pleasure.

Acknowledge our needs,
the hard ones and the fun ones,
holding both our gifts and challenges.
And let sweet peach juice drip down our chins.

Remember

Remember, dear one.
Remember before they told you that you weren't right,
or enough,
or too much.

Remember when you came into being.
A spark of life,
born of a miracle,
of this egg, this sperm, that moment.
You were chosen by celestial timing,
your DNA from your grandmothers' eggs.
Made up of the constellation and elements of the very
    stars.

Remember when you ran wild,
talked to the trees,
and frogs,
and dolls.
Built stick forts in the woods, and blanket forts in the
    bedroom,
and you loved your own company.

Remember when you made sure not one of your dolls was
    left out
because you loved them all, and they needed you.

Remember wonder.
Watching butterflies hatch,
and pondering the link between tadpoles and frogs.
Fascinated to find hearts, and stomachs, and eggs when
    cleaning fish.
Sitting with friends on the braided rug
while the librarian shared stories of adventures in magical
    places.

Moaning when it was time to pause the story,
begging for more.
Reading under the covers by flashlight,
sure that you have fooled your parents.

Remember mastery.
Skipping a rock.
The day your body knew how to do a headstand, and a
    cartwheel.
The time you took a deep breath and flew across the river,
and didn't get a speck of wet.
The time the bike finally obeyed your feet,
and you joined the world of riders.
You chose to ride in zig zags all over the street,
because straight lines just weren't you.

Remember, dear one, this is all with you still.
Even if you forgot, or they told you differently.

Make a memory today for that wild and wonderful you
whom you forgot,
in homage to the stardust that you are.

Finds Joy

For me, joy is often fleeting like a hummingbird.
A flash of beauty and then it's gone.
Yet it's always been there,
often unnoticed under chores,
pain
loneliness
survival.

It shows up in the dappled sunlight of the back yard
head in the shade,
legs in the sun.
Steller's Jays making soft chittering sounds I've never
    heard before.
Usually, I only hear them scream.
Are they speaking to their babies?
Are they relaxed too?

Joy arrives in laughter when someone "gets me."
Often the laughter is dark humor;
how wonderful to find joy in managing distress together.
An occupational hazard.

While I write this poem, a graduation parade goes by
honking and yelling.
Usually, I loathe the intrusion of noise in my backyard
    respite,
but this noise heralds accomplishments and new
beginnings.
Teachers and students finished the year in spite of the
pandemic's obstacles and losses.
I don't know the revelers, but for right now
we share joy.

Everything has its shadow,
but no shadow without light.

I remember my name,
Finds Joy.

Reimagining Wild Things

Max grew up still wearing his wolf suit.
He believed it to be necessary to tame wild and scary
    things.
One night Max woke to his deepest intention
to be present to his own life.
No longer suspending joy.
He unzipped the suit and stepped out into his world.
Unstrapped the weights around his ankles
and left behind the cement shoes of history.
Present with what is:
The wild things and the simple things.
The feel of the breeze.
The nip and kisses from the cat, even at 2am.
The gift and taste of food.
The rhythm of walking.
The connection of souls.
To walk in presence and belonging,
leaving the costume crumpled on the floor as a reminder
of the alternative.
Let the wild rumpus begin!

Citations

Look Up
https://poets.org/poem/day

The Moon Won't Use the Door
https://www.goodreads.com/quotes/629973-there-is-some-kiss-we-want-with-our-whole-lives

Only Writing Does Writing
Writing Down the Bones, 2005 by Natalie Goldberg (p. 12)

A Prayer for Those Without Words
Mary Oliver, *Thirst*
https://www.goodreads.com/quotes/414333-praying-it-doesn-t-have-to-be-the-blue-iris-it

Reimagining Wild Things
"Let the Wild Rumpus Start"
Sendak, Maurice. (1983). *Where the Wild Things Are.* Scholastic INC. (p. 22)

Rigged
https://www.facebook.com/AnneLamott/posts/318393946315785

That Unnoticed and That Necessary
From *Selected Poems II: 1976-1986* by Margaret Atwood.

Acknowledgments

Let Yourself Be Weary won the 2022 Sue C. Boynton Poetry Award.

Peace in the Eye of the Storm was featured in the Writing Together, Rising Together People's Perspective Project in 2020.
https://www.villagebooks.com/event/litlive-peoples-perspectives-091020

ABOUT THE AUTHOR

Maureen Sandra Kane lives in Bellingham, WA with her husband and hairless cat, Luna. She is a mental health therapist in private practice. Prior to being a therapist, she focused her work on literacy, health care access, aging, homeless youth, and disability.

Maureen is a winner of the 2022 Sue C. Boynton Poetry Award, and her work has been featured in the Writing Together, Rising Together People's Perspective Project.

Made in the USA
Monee, IL
07 May 2022